DIRT BIKES

BY LINDSAY SHAFFER

BELLWETHER MEDIA • MINNEAPOLIS, MN

EPIC

EPIC BOOKS are no ordinary books. They burst with intense action, high-speed heroics, and shadows of the unknown. Are you ready for an Epic adventure?

This edition first published in 2019 by Bellwether Media, Inc.

No part of this publication may be reproduced in whole or in part without written permission of the publisher. For information regarding permission, write to Bellwether Media, Inc., Attention: Permissions Department, 6012 Blue Circle Drive, Minnetonka, MN 55343.

Library of Congress Cataloging-in-Publication Data

Names: Shaffer, Lindsay, author.
Title: Dirt Bikes / by Lindsay Shaffer.
Description: Minneapolis, MN : Bellwether Media, Inc., 2019. | Series: Epic. Full Throttle | Includes bibliographical references and index. | Audience: Ages 7-12. | Audience: Grades 2 to 7.
Identifiers: LCCN 2018002180 (print) | LCCN 2018008164 (ebook) | ISBN 9781626178717 (hardcover : alk. paper) | ISBN 9781681036182 (ebook)
Subjects: LCSH: Trail bikes–Juvenile literature.
Classification: LCC TL441 (ebook) | LCC TL441 .S529 2019 (print) | DDC 629.227/2-dc23
LC record available at https://lccn.loc.gov/2018002180

Editor: Christina Leaf   Designer: Jeffrey Kollock

Printed in the United States of America, North Mankato, MN

TABLE OF CONTENTS

X GAMES GOLD!

Dirt bike rider Levi Sherwood speeds toward a steep ramp. He is competing in the freestyle event at the 2017 X Games. Sherwood launches off the ramp and does a double backflip before landing. The crowd cheers!

Sherwood circles back toward the ramp. He does a few more midair tricks.

GET CREATIVE!
Freestyle riders often create their own tricks. They love to surprise the crowd!

Then, he wows the crowd with another double backflip. Sherwood wins the gold medal!

WHAT ARE DIRT BIKES?

Dirt bikes are a type of motorcycle used for riding off-road. They have light frames and bumpy tires. Dirt bikes can race through muddy, sandy, or rocky terrain. They squeeze through tight turns and fly over large jumps.

HIT THE GYM!

Dirt bike riders must be strong and physically fit.

People ride dirt bikes on outdoor trails and in competitions. Some families enjoy riding together.

New riders can take classes to learn how to ride safely. Some classes teach tricks, too!

Riders wear helmets, goggles, and padded clothing. This gear protects them if they fall.

11

THE HISTORY OF DIRT BIKES

In the early 1900s, motorized bikes became popular in Europe. They looked like bicycles with small engines. People rode them both on and off-road. They raced them, too!

1918 motorized bike

1909 motorized bike

DIRT BIKE TIMELINE

The first official cross-country motorcycle race takes place in Great Britain

1924

1959

Honda creates and markets "trail bikes" as a new type of motorcycle

1972

First American Motorcycle Association Motocross Championship is held

Over time, off-road motorcycles became known as dirt bikes. A company called Honda helped make dirt bikes popular in the United States. Today, many people ride for fun or compete in motocross.

DIRT BIKE PARTS

Dirt bikes are small, light, and tough. They have powerful suspension systems. Suspension systems keep the ride smooth and stop the tires from bouncing after jumps. They use large metal springs or air shocks.

suspension system

MAKE IT PERSONAL!

Many riders make their dirt bikes stand out by covering them with stickers.

fender

Bumpy tires provide good traction for dirt bikes. Plastic fenders protect riders from mud and water that spray from the wheels.

Handlebars hold several important parts. Turning the throttle sends fuel to the engine. Pulling the clutch lever shifts gears.

IDENTIFY A DIRT BIKE

throttle

clutch

fender

light frame

suspension system

bumpy tires

brakes

DIRT BIKE COMPETITIONS

FLYING HIGH

In 2012, Alex Harvill set a new record. He jumped his dirt bike 425 feet (129.5 meters). This is the longest motorcycle jump ever!

freestyle

Riders across the world compete in races including motocross and enduro. Enduro races may last seven hours or more! In freestyle competitions, riders perform special tricks. Riders look forward to each new adventure!

enduro

GLOSSARY

air shocks—parts of a suspension system that use air to cushion the ride; air shocks are lighter than metal springs.

clutch—the part that allows a dirt bike to shift gears

competitions—contests

enduro—long-distance dirt bike races with many natural obstacles

fenders—coverings over the wheels that block splashing

freestyle—a type of competition in which riders do special tricks for points

motocross—outdoor motocycle races on rough, dirt paths

motorized—having a motor

off-road—on trails or dirt roads

suspension systems—systems of springs, tires, and shocks that cushion a vehicle's ride

terrain—land

throttle—the part that controls fuel going to an engine

traction—the ability to grip a surface while moving

TO LEARN MORE

AT THE LIBRARY

Lanier, Wendy Hinote. *Dirt Bikes*. Lake Elmo, Minn.: Focus Readers, 2017.

Polydoros, Lori. *Dirt Bike Racing*. North Mankato, Minn.: Capstone Press, 2014.

Shaffer, Lindsay. *Motocross Cycles*. Minneapolis, Minn.: Bellwether Media, 2019.

ON THE WEB

Learning more about dirt bikes is as easy as 1, 2, 3.

1. Go to www.factsurfer.com.

2. Enter "dirt bikes" into the search box.

3. Click the "Surf" button and you will see a list of related web sites.

With factsurfer.com, finding more information is just a click away.

INDEX